LAB MANUAL TO ACCOMPANY

THE OBJECT CONCEPT

An Introduction to Computer Programming Using C++

RICK DECKER
STUART HIRSHFIELD
Hamilton College

PWS Publishing Company

I(T)P International Thomson Publishing Company

Boston • Albany • Bonn • Cincinnati • Detroit • London • Madrid
Melbourne • Mexico City • New York • Paris • San Francisco
Singapore • Tokyo • Toronto • Washington

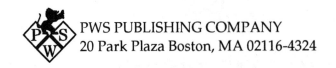

PWS PUBLISHING COMPANY
20 Park Plaza Boston, MA 02116-4324

I ⊤ P™
International Thomson Publishing
The trademark ITP is used under license.

For more information, contact:

PWS Publishing Co.
20 Park Plaza
Boston, MA 02116

International Thomson Publishing Europe
Berkshire House I68–I73
High Holborn
London WC1V 7AA
England

Thomas Nelson Australia
102 Dodds Street
South Melbourne, 3205
Victoria, Australia

Nelson Canada
1120 Birchmount Road
Scarborough, Ontario
Canada M1K 5G4

International Thomson Editores
Campos Eliseos 385, Piso 7
Col. Polanco
11560 Mexico D.F., Mexico

International Thomson Publishing GmbH
Königswinterer Strasse 418
53227 Bonn, Germany

International Thomson Publishing Asia
221 Henderson Road
#05–10 Henderson Building
Singapore 0315

International Thomson Publishing Japan
Hirakawacho Kyowa Building, 31
2-2-1 Hirakawacho
Chiyoda-ku, Tokyo 102
Japan

ISBN 0-534-20500-3

Printed and bound in the United States of America.
95 96 97 98 99—10 9 8 7 6 5 4 3 2 1

Contents

Preface

In *The Object Concept,* we say that one of the key pedagogical features of this package is its reliance on directed laboratory exercises as the primary vehicle for learning. This manual reflects that distinct orientation. Where the text provides descriptions of abstract principles (the C++ language and object-oriented programming techniques), the lab exercises provide a means for active experimentation that renders the concepts developed in the text tangible and meaningful to students. Indeed, we view the text as a supplement to this manual, not the other way around.

Each of the lab sessions (one per chapter of the text) begins with a brief description of the programming and C++ language concepts to be addressed, a review of the Program in Progress (PIP) that illustrates these concepts, and a listing of specific lab objectives. The exercises that follow typically begin with instructions to run the PIP, which provides the point of departure for subsequent exercises. (As a result, students spend less time typing, and more time programming.) Most of the exercises involve modifying, testing, and expanding the PIP in specific ways that require an understanding of the programming and language-specific concepts involved. Some of the exercises are more exploratory in that they encourage students to conceive and/or perform a test that tells them something about C++. Finally, "Postlab Exercises" provided at the end of each lab may require students to develop the PIP even further, or to apply the same principles demonstrated in the PIP to an altogether new problem. We use these Postlab Exercises as a source of homework assignments.

In adopting this lab-based approach we make no explicit assumptions about how a course is organized. Indeed, all of the following arrangements have worked well for us:

- "Closed," scheduled lab sessions with the instructor and teaching assistants available for help;
- More flexibly scheduled "open" lab sessions, with a teaching assistant available for consultation;

- No scheduled lab sessions at all, where we rely on students to complete the labs on their own. This is clearly the least desirable format, as it requires that teaching assistants be available on a regular basis to help students with questions about their particular programming environment.

All that matters is that the lab exercises get done during, before, or after (in our order of preference) the class in which the corresponding text chapter is covered. Each set of exercises (excluding the Postlab exercises) is designed to take from one to three hours of time "at the machine," depending upon the student's preparation and the amount of experimentation that they choose to conduct.

A Final Word about the Computer Environment

Before beginning the labs, a quick word is in order about programming environments. This lab manual, the exercises it contains, and the PIPs it refers to are as "generic" as we could make them. That is, they were not written with a specific implementation of C++ in mind. Our intention was to provide sample programs and exercises that could be run in many different environments. Toward that end, the PIPs have been encoded on the accompanying disk as straight text files that can be transferred to and opened from many different C++ implementations. Further, we have done our best to avoid using compiler-specific code, and when we had no choice, we documented the PIP clearly to indicate that a particular statement or function call may require modification to run in a specific environment. Ideally, this manual could be supplemented with either manuals for your compiler, or (better still) with more directed handouts that describe features of the environment that you want your students to make use of. We know from direct personal experience that all of the PIPs work, and that all of the exercises can be accomplished using Borland's Turbo C++, Borland C++, and Symantec's THINK C++.

If you have a compiler and our lab disk, and if you have read that portion of Chapter 1 of the text that describes the first PIP, you are ready to begin the first lab. Enjoy!

Chapter 1
Designing with Classes

Introduction

This set of lab exercises is somewhat different from those that will follow in at least three important ways. First of all, out of necessity it focuses on using the your C++ programming environment as opposed to the C++ language per se. We must get through these "system" preliminaries in order for you to begin developing your programming expertise in subsequent chapters. Second, whereas most labs will begin with a Program in Progress (PIP) that is described in the text, in this case you don't yet know enough C++ to make much sense of the program. Not to worry— we'll guide you through it so that you can make it work and understand its output. Finally, in all other labs you are provided with a copy of the PIP as the starting point for your lab exercises. Given that the primary purpose of this chapter's lab is to show you how to use your C++ system to create working programs, you begin this lab on your own. Start by typing in your first C++ program.

Lab Objectives

In this lab, you will:
- Become familiar with your C++ programming environment.
- Learn how to enter, edit, run, and save C++ programs.
- Gain experience fixing C++ syntax errors.
- Investigate the program libraries that are available in your C++ environment.

Exercises

1. As we described in Chapter 1 of the text, C++ programs tend to be composed of many files. According to our Declare-Define-Use approach for developing programs, we will normally create separate files for class declarations (header files with ".H" extensions), class definitions (implementations files with ".CPP" extensions), and class usage (program files containing function `main`). The PIP for Chapter 1 conforms to this standard. It is comprised of three files, named "DIGITIME.H", "DIGITIME.CPP", and "PIP1.CPP", all listed below.

As we mentioned earlier, in all subsequent chapters your lab disk will contain copies of all files that comprise the PIP. In Chapter 1, however, it is up to you to enter the PIP on your own. Your job in this set of exercises is to enter all three files into your C++ system, to compile them, to link them to form a runnable program, and to run the PIP.

Your instructor will provide you with the details of using your particular C++ pro-gramming environment for entering, editing, and saving files. Once you have access to a computer and have been told how to start and use C++, perform the following tasks.

```
//-------------- DIGITIME.H --------------

// Declarations of classes Display and Timer


class Display
// A Display object stores and displays a single integer.
// That integer is always in the range 0 .. limit-1, where limit
// is also stored in the class.
{
public:
    Display(int lim);           // Initialize a new Display object

    void Increment();           // Add 1 to value
    void SetValue(int val);     // Set the value
```

```
   int GetValue();            // Return the current value
   void Show();               // Show the current value
   int GetLimit();            // Return the limit

private:
   int    limit,              // largest possible value
          value;              // current value (0 .. limit - 1)
};


class Timer
// A Timer object consists of two Displays, one for hours
// and one for minutes. When the timer is incremented
// and minutes becomes 60, minutes is reset to 0
// and hours is incremented.
{
public:
   Timer();        // Initialize a new Timer object,
                   // setting max hours to 24 and max minutes to 60
   void Increment();    // Add 1 minute to timer
   void Set();          // Set hours and minutes
   void Show();         // Show hours and minutes
private:
   Display  hours,      // two displays, one for hours,
            minutes;    // and one for minutes
};



//------------- DIGITIME.CPP -------------

#include <iostream.h>      // for cout, cin
#include "DIGITIME.H"      // for Display and Timer declarations


//------------- Definition of member functions for class Display

Display::Display(int lim)
// Initialize a new Display object.
{
   value = 0;
   limit = lim;
}
```

```
void Display::Increment()
// Add 1 to value.  If incrementing makes value
// equal to limit, reset value to zero.
{
   value++;
   if (value == limit)
      value = 0;
}

void Display::SetValue(int val)
// Set the value.
// If the argument is negative, we make it positive.
// To make sure value is within the right range, we set the value
// to its remainder upon division by limit.
{
   if (val < 0)
      val = -val;
   value = (val % limit);
}

int Display::GetValue()
// Return the current value.
{
   return value;
}

void Display::Show()
// Show the value of a Display.
{
   if (value < 10)           // Pad with a leading zero, if needed,
      cout << '0';

   cout << value;            // and in any case, display the value.
}

int Display::GetLimit()
// Return the limit for this Display.
{
   return limit;
}
```

```
//-------------- Definition of member functions for class Timer

Timer::Timer() : hours(24), minutes(60)
// Initialize a new Timer object,
// setting hours limit to 24 and minutes limit to 60.
{
    // All the work is done by the two constructor calls
    // in the header.
}

void Timer::Increment()
// Add 1 minute to timer.
{
    minutes.Increment();

    if (minutes.GetValue() == 0)
        // We've turned the minute counter over,
        hours.Increment();
        // so we have to increment the hours counter.
}

void Timer::Set()
// Set hours and minutes from the keyboard.
{
    int setting;                 // user-input values for hours,
minutes

    cout << "Set hours to what value?\n";
    cout << "Enter an integer between 0 and " <<
            hours.GetLimit() << ": ";
    cin >> setting;
    hours.SetValue(setting);     // Set hours.

    cout << "Set minutes to what value?\n";
    cout << "Enter an integer between 0 and " <<
            minutes.GetLimit() << ": ";
    cin >> setting;
    minutes.SetValue(setting);   // Set minutes.
}

void Timer::Show()
// Show the current timer's settings.
```

```
{
    hours.Show();
    cout << ':';
    minutes.Show();
}


//-------------- PIP1.CPP --------------

#include <iostream.h>        // for cout, cin
#include "DIGITIME.H"        // for our Timer and Display classes

void main()
{
    Timer t;      // Create and initialize a Timer object, named "t."

    cout << "Here's the initial value of the timer: ";
    t.Show();
    cout << "\n\n";

    t.Set();      // Allow the user to set the timer's value.
    cout << "Here are the new settings: ";
    t.Show();
    cout << "\n\n";

    cout << "Now we run it for ten minutes . . .\n";

    for (int i = 0; i < 10; i++)
    {
        t.Increment();
        t.Show();
        cout << '\n';
    }

    // Freeze the screen until the user presses a key.
    cout << "\nPress any key and ENTER to conclude processing: ";
    char any;
    cin >> any;
    cout << "\nPROCESSING COMPLETED ... GOOD BYE";
}
```

 a. Type the contents of file "DIGITIME.H" exactly as it appears, above.

 b. Save the file as "DIGITIME.H".

 c. Compile file "DIGITIME.H".

 d. Correct any syntax errors detected by the C++ compiler by editing the offending line(s).

 e. Repeat steps (c) and (d) until your file compiles successfully.

 f. Enter, save, compile, and edit file"DIGITIME.CPP", as above.

 g. Enter, save, compile, and edit file"PIP1.CPP", as above.

2. Now that all three of the files for the PIP have been successfully compiled (translated into machine language), your program can be run. In order to run PIP1, though, the three compiled files must be combined into a single collection of machine language code. In most implementations of C++, this is accomplished by "linking" the programs.

 a. Check with your instructor to determine the procedure for linking a program in your version of C++, and follow it.

 b. Run PIP1. When asked to provide values for *hours* and *minutes*, do so by typing an integer, and hitting the Return or Enter key.

 c. Run PIP1 again, this time with the program listing opened next to you. See if you can determine which parts of the program produce which output on the screen.

3. For all subsequent chapters, every lab will contain exercises that ask you to extend the PIP to describe some additional information or to perform some additional processing. Usually, these exercises require that you do some programming on your own. Clearly, we're not quite ready for that here in Chapter 1, so like we did in the first PIP, we will provide you with the code needed to extend our digital time in a simple way. As with the original PIP, you may or may not understand the code itself—don't worry about that for now. We view the following as exercises in using your C++ environment to edit, compile, link, and run C++ programs, and so should you.

a. Edit the file "DIGITIME.H" as follows. (If your environment allows cutting, copying, and pasting of text, these operations will come in handy here.)

   (1) Add the following line to the class *Display* declaration after the line that reads*void Increment( );*

```
void Decrement();
```

   (2) Add the following line to the class *Timer* declaration after the line that reads*void Increment( );*

```
void Decrement();
```

b. Compile file "DIGITIME.H". Repeat the editing steps in (a), above, until the file compiles successfully.

c. Edit the file "DIGITIME.CPP" as follows. Add the following function definitions to the file. They can be added anywhere in the file after the include directives, so long as they don't interfere with any of the other definitions in the file.

```
void Display::Decrement()
{
    if (value == 0)
        value=limit-1;
    else
        value--;
```

```
    }

    void Timer::Decrement()
    {
        minutes.Decrement();
        if (minutes.GetValue() == (minutes.GetLimit() - 1))
            hours.Decrement();
    }
```

d. Compile and continue editing file "DIGITIME.CPP" until all C++ syntax errors have been eliminated.

e. Edit file "PIP1.CPP" to include the lines below. Enter these lines before the comment line in the original that begins "// Freeze the screen...". Again, note the repeated lines of code here, and use your program editor to save some typing.

```
t.Set();
cout << "Here are the new settings: ";
t.Show();
cout << "\n\n";

cout << "Now we run it for ten minutes BACKWARDS. . .\n";

for (int j = 0; j < 10; j++)
{
    t.Decrement();
    t.Show();
    cout << '\n';
}
```

f. Compile and continue editing file "PIP1.CPP" until all C++ syntax errors have been eliminated.

g. Link your edited files together, and run the revised version of the PIP.

h. As before, run the program a few times and see if you can determine which parts of the new program are producing which output on the screen. In particular, try any or all of the following when you are asked by the program to set the time. See if you can use file "DIGITIME.CPP" to explain the program's behavior.

(1) set one of the values to a negative number

(2) set the hours value to 26

(3) set the time to 11:59

(4) set the time to 23:55

(5) set the time to 00:05

Postlab Exercises

1. Look ahead in the text to the Chapter 2 PIP. (Again, don't worry about what it does!) Enter, compile, edit, and run it using your C++ environment.

2. All C++ environments come equipped with a collection of built-in program libraries, containing declarations and definitions of many useful classes for building programs. Many environments allow you to "browse" through the libraries on-line (that is, form within the C++ environment). Ask your instructor if and how you can gain access to your C++ library files. Use any available on-line "help" to browse through them. If nothing else, this will give you a feeling for the variety of built-in classes that C++ provides for you.

Chapter 2
The Ingredients of Classes

Introduction

From this point on in our lab sessions our emphasis will shift from using the C++ programming environment to understanding and using the C++ language to describe and solve problems—that is, we will concentrate on the programming language and process. In this and all subsequent labs the Program in Progress (PIP) will serve as our starting and ending points. It provides us with both a vehicle for C++ experimentation, and a source of programming building blocks— "reusable code" in C++ parlance—which we will make use of in other programs.

The Chapter 2 PIP, as described in the text, provides us with a class that implements fractions. The PIP makes use of a variety of simple C++ data type and operators, and defines some simple functions of its own. We will use it to investigate these basic ingredients of all C++ programs.

Lab Objectives

In this lab, you will:
- Run and analyze the behavior of the Chapter 2 PIP, *Fraction*, paying particular attention to its use of C++ atomic data type, operators, and functions.
- Modify the PIP to produce a variety of C++ compiler, linker, and runtime errors.
- Extend the *Fraction* class to include additional operators.

Exercises

1 . Before we set you off to do some programming of your own, we will walk you through this chapter's PIP pointing out many of the C++ features we introduced in the text. Since we covered a wide range of topics in the text, we'll use a shotgun approach to analyzing the PIP.

All of the items below describe editing tasks we want you to perform on the original versions of some of the files involved in our PIP ("FRACTION.H", "FRACTION.CPP", and "PIP2.CPP"). For each editing task, your job is to describe the error that results (if one does!) from the change we asked you to make to the PIP. That is, write down on a separate sheet of paper the error message produced, the offending line(s) of the file, your guess as to the cause of the error, and whether the error was detected when compiling, linking, or running your program. If no error was produced, indicate this and describe why the program still runs.

You should proceed as follows: First, change the appropriate file as described. Then, try compiling the file that was edited. If it still compiles successfully, try linking the program. If that works, run the program and note its behavior.

Start out by saving backup copies of the original version of the three files mentioned above. You can use these as the starting point for each editing exercise below. For each exercise, the name of the file to be edited appears in parentheses.

a. ("FRACTION.H") Remove any comment symbol ("//").

b. ("FRACTION.H") Add a comment symbol at the start of the line that begins *Fraction();*

c. ("FRACTION.H") Remove any ";" .

d. ("FRACTION.H") Change the line that reads *Fraction (int n, int d=1);* to: *Fraction (int n, d=1);*

e. ("FRACTION.H") Remove the line that begins *void Get();*.

f. ("PIP2.CPP") Change the line that reads *Fraction f1(3,2), f2(4), f3;* to: *Fraction f1(3,2), f2(4);*

g. ("FRACTION.CPP") Remove all parentheses from the statement that begins *r.numerator = ...* in the definition of operator +.

h. ("FRACTION.CPP") Change the final line of function *Fraction::Evaluate()* to read *return (n div d).*

i. ("FRACTION.CPP") Add the line cout << r after the line numerator = n; in function *Fraction::Fraction(int n, int d)*.

j. ("FRACTION.H") Move the line that begins *double Evaluate()...* so that it is the last line (before the final "}") of class *Fraction*.

k. ("FRACTION.H") Remove the characters "= 1" from the line that begins *Fraction(int n, int d=1);*

l. ("FRACTION.CPP") Remove the line that begins *return r* from operator +.

2. Now, let's extend our PIP (using, of course, the original versions of all files) to perform some additional operations. It would be nice, obviously, to extend our class definition of *Fraction* to allow fractions to be subtracted from one another. Doing so involves three steps—declaring, defining, and using our new operator (surprise!).

a. First, add a declaration to the *Fraction* class declaration describing a new operator, "-". (Use the + operator declaration as a model.) Compile the header file successfully before proceeding.

b. Now, use the definition of the + operator in file "FRACTION.CPP" to write a definition for your new subtraction operator. Compile the implementation file before proceeding.

c. Finally, add to file "PIP2.CPP" statements that will test your operator, and display the results of a subtraction operation.

Repeat the above steps until your subtraction operator works as it should.

3. Extend the PIP as in exercise 2 to overload the multiplication (*) and division (/) operators for class *Fraction*.

Postlab Exercises

1. Think of a simple problem that could make use of your extended *Fraction* class (how about as compound interest calculation, or a program that performs English-to-metric conversions). Write a new `main` function that uses your class to solve the problem.

2. Design, declare, define, and test a class implementation of complex numbers.

Chapter 3
Class Actions I: Selection Statements

Introduction

Just as Chapters 3 and 4 in the text combine to describe the major control structures of C++, the corresponding PIPs combine to create a single program which simulates a soda machine and provides the means for a user to interact with the simulated machine. In fact, you need (and have on your disk) all of the files from Chapters 3 and 4 to actually run this PIP. Don't worry about the contents of the files from Chapter 4 for now. They implement the user interface part of the program and make use of some C++ features that we haven't discussed yet. One of the beauties of C++, as you saw back in Chapter 1, is that you can use files that support your program without having to understand them in any detail.

In this lab, we'll concentrate on the details of our soda machine description, as embodied in class *Machine*. You will see how a variety of C++ control structures are used to allow the program to make decisions while it is running. We will also look carefully at the communication aspects of describing such a machine. That is, we will trace the actions of the soda machine as its internal objects invoke and respond to messages that are initiated by users and/or other parts of the machine.

Lab Objectives

In this lab, you will:
- Run and trace the processing action of the Chapter 3 PIP, a soda machine

simulation.
- Analyze the PIP, paying special attention to the C++ selection statements used to describe its actions.
- Experiment with and revise some of the class definitions to perform additional types of selection.
- Extend the description of the soda machine to allow it to accept silver dollars, and to handle change more realistically.
- See firsthand how a C++ program designed according to our Declare-Define-Use approach is easy to extend and revise.

Exercises

1. We will start this lab, as usual, by running the PIP in its original form. The Chapter 3 PIP is somewhat more interesting in this regard because you, just like the user of a soda machine, have a great deal of control over how the program runs. Depending upon what coins you insert and which buttons you push, the soda machine/program will respond differently. In some cases it will dispense a soda, and in other its response will be no response at all (for example, if you push a button choosing a soda without having inserted any coins). Let's try to get a feel for how the program responds to various inputs.

   a. Start by compiling, linking, and running PIP 3. Provide whatever responses you want to the program's prompts. Do your best to exercise as many of its features as you can. Then, on a separate sheet of paper, write down the names of every member function from class *Machine* that you think gets invoked as the program reacts to your responses.

   b. Now, run the PIP again, entering the following responses to its prompts:

Q	to insert a quarter
Q	insert another quarter
C	press the cola button
D	insert a dime
D	insert another dime
N	insert a nickel

B   press the root beer selector button
X   walk away from the machine (exit the program)

c. Re-run the program in the exact same way, but as you do, write down on a separate sheet of paper the name of each member function from class *Machine* that gets invoked as it gets invoked. NOTE: If your C++ programming environment provides facilities for "stepping through" or "tracing" the action of a program, this would be a good time to ask your instructor about them. If you have no automated support for this task, do it by hand. Print copies of the files that describe class *Machine*, and use them as a guide for following the program's actions.

d. See how your first, informal list of function names compares with the second, more detailed list. If you were careful in recoding function names, your final list probably includes every function defined in every one of the PIP's files. Even if you missed a few (did you include the constructor functions for class *Dispenser* and class *CoinCounter*?), you should now have a good feel for the basic flow of processing control within the PIP.

2. Now, we'll ask you to make a couple of changes to the original version of the PIP so as to experiment with its use of C++ selection statements. The good news is that each of these changes is localized to a particular function definition, and demonstrates an interesting feature of C++. The bad news is that we're not going to tell you how to make the changes. It's up to you to begin exercising your growing programming expertise. For each change below, you should: edit the appropriate file to reflect your solution, compile and link your program, run the revised program, and check out its behavior. In each case, it should perform as did the original. If it doesn't, repeat the process with a new "fix."

After modifying the program successfully, answer the question about it.[1]

a. In function *SodaMachine::DoCoin*, change all `break` statements to

---

1 It is always a good idea, whether we tell you to or not, to save the original version of each PIP so that you can refer or revert to it as needed. In general, you should make copies of all program files, and should work from those copies in lab.

`return` statements. Q: Why does the function work with either type of statement?

b. Split function *SodaMachine::DoSelection* into two. That is, define a function, *SodaMachine::MakeSale*, that embodies the attempted sale of any brand of soda, and rewrite *DoSelection* to call *MakeSale*. Q: Is there an advantage to defining a separate *MakeSale* function?

3. You can use either the original program files or your revised files from the previous exercises as the starting point for these exercises. Here, we ask you to extend the PIP in more substantive ways. Both of these extensions involve changing declarations as well as definitions, but—interestingly enough—do not dictate any change to function `main`. Also, whereas the changes are more extensive than those you made in exercise 2, they are still well-defined and easily made given the organization of our program. You will see that the combination of C++ and the Declare-Define-Use approach allows a program to be extended in interesting ways without having to start over. This, after all, is what good program design is all about.

For each of these extensions, write the required code, compile each file involved separately, link, and run the program. Test it until you are convinced that it works. Then, ask one of your classmates to run your program to see if any errors turn up that you didn't anticipate. You should complete part **a** before attempting part **b**.

a. Alter the machine so that it accepts single dollars. Assume for now that dollars are inserted through the existing coin counter (i.e., they are silver dollars).

b. In running your revised program you may have noticed a shortcoming of our original. When one of our soda machines runs out of coins to make change with, it displays a message telling the user "EXACT CHANGE ONLY from now on ...". Unfortunately, after doing so it takes the user's money, dispenses a soda, and does not return any change. Most real soda machines in similar situations don't keep the money or dispense a soda unless the exact amount has actually been provided. Fix our program to operate in this more realistic fashion.

Postlab Exercises

1. Change the soda machine so that it accepts dollar bills, and does so through a separate "bill counter" (as opposed to the existing coin counter).

2. Write an English critique of how well our C++ description of a soda machine matches a real machine. Discuss, for example, what assumptions we have made about the type of machine being modelled. Are there soda machines that you are familiar with that are not accurately described by our program? If we wanted our program to provide a more in-depth description of such a machine, how could the program be extended?

Chapter 4
Class Actions II: Repetition Statements

Introduction

This lab picks up right where the Chapter 3 lab left off, by continuing our exploration of the soda machine PIP. In this chapter, though, we'll concentrate on the user interface part of the program as that is where we make extensive use of C++'s repetition statements. The fact that both the user interface portions of the program and the free functions we have described in our "Utility" files are critically dependent on C++'s ability to express repetition is testimony to the power and general usefulness of iteration.

Both of the classes involved in this PIP illustrate these properties. Each uses a variety of loops to describe an interesting, non-trivial problem. Each is also readily extensible to a more general class of problems. Just as the *Machine* class can be generalized to describe a wider range of vending machines, our *User* class can be modified ever so slightly to produce a variety of menu-based user interfaces. In this lab we'll review the behavior of the *User* class, and then see how the two classes combine to form a complete program.

Lab Objectives

In this lab, you will:
- Run and trace the processing action of the *User* class in the Chapter 4 PIP.
- Analyze the PIP, paying special attention to the repetition statements used to

describe its actions.
- Experiment with and revise some of the loops.
- Extend the description of the soda machine to allow it to dispense additional soda types and to accept paper currency.

Exercises

1. This lab is similar to the Chapter 3 lab in format as well as in content. We'll follow pretty much the same steps in analyzing our PIP, except that in this run through we will focus on class *User*, and its use of repetition statements.

    a. Start as we did in Chapter 3 by compiling, linking, and running PIP 4. In this case, let's do our best to exercise and trace the actions of the user interface to our soda machine. Run the program, and provide the following sequence of input characters (one at a time) when prompted.

Q	to insert a quarter
C	press the cola selector button
q	insert another quarter (using a lowercase character)
Z	illegal command
m	show the menu using a lowercase character
e	another illegal command
Q	to insert another quarter
2	another illegal character (this time it's also a number)
B	press the root beer selector button
X	walk away from the machine (exit the program)

    b. How many times do you think each of the following statements was executed during the course of the interaction described above? You can figure it out by looking carefully at the code listing, or you can use any automated support provided by your C++ environment for tracing the action of a program.

(1) the `if` statement in function `main`

(2) the `return` statement in function *User::IsLegal*

(3 the call to function *ShowMenu* from within function
User::GetCommand

2 . Now, as before, we'll ask you to make some changes to the original version of
the PIP so that you can experiment with its use of repetition statements. Edit
the appropriate file to reflect your solution, compile and link your program, run
the revised program, and check out its behavior. In each case, it should
perform as did the original. If it doesn't, repeat the process with a new "fix."
After modifying the program successfully, answer the question about it.

a . In function *User::GetCommand*, rewrite the `while` loop so that its
expression more directly controls the exit from the loop. That is, rewrite the
function so that it does not make use of a potentially infinite loop. Q:
Which version of the loop is easier for you to understand? Why?

b . In function `main`, rewrite the `do` loop to be a `while` loop. Q: Is there a
reason in this example to prefer one loop type over the other?

3 . You can use either the original program files or your revised files from the
previous exercises as the starting point for these exercises. Here, we ask you to
extend the PIP in more substantive ways. For each of these extensions, write
the required code, compile each file involved separately, link, and run the
program. Test it until you are convinced that it works. As before, ask one of
your classmates to run your program to see if they can turn up any errors you
didn't anticipate.

a . Add a new dispenser, for ginger ale, to the soda machine.

b. Change the PIP so that it can process many customers. That is, embed the `while` loop in function `main` within another loop that allows all processing to be repeated any number of times. You can use function *ReadyToQuit* from our "UTILITY" library to control exit from the new, outer loop.

Postlab Exercises

1. Modify class *User* so that it serves as the interface to:

    a. a vending machine that dispenses candy, gum, and chips.
    b. a microwave oven.
    c. an automated teller machine (ATM).

2. Use class *Machine* as a model to write a program that describes a more general vending machine class. That is, write a class description of a machine that could equally well be used to model a soda, candy, or ice cream machine.

Chapter 5
Compound Data

Introduction

The PIP for this chapter is a card-playing program which, given the fact that it is comprised of seven separate C++ files, seems more complex than any of the previous PIPs. What you'll see in this lab is that we have exploited C++'s ability to describe complex system in terms of simple, cooperating classes, and that the resulting code is remarkably readable and straightforward. The program is made all the more readable by our ability to describe and manipulate compound objects—that is, objects with parts that themselves are interesting (like a deck of cards)—directly in C++.

In the exercises that follow we will investigate both the C++ language features that the PIP makes use of and the PIP's design. Specifically, we will concentrate on the program's use of arrays and classes, and on how the Deck, Player, and Dealer classes interact to produce a working, extensible program.

Lab Objectives

In this lab, you will:
- Use this chapter's PIP, a card-playing program, to experiment with C++ arrays and classes.
- Write a "driver program" that allows you to perform incremental testing on the PIP.

- Modify the PIP to use additional C++ compound data.
- Extend the PIP so that it serves as a more general model for card games.

Exercises

1. We'll begin by using our PIP to analyze some features of C++ that are new to this chapter. As before, we suggest that you start by making backup copies of all files so that you can use the original version for subsequent exercises. In each case, make the suggested change, and compile, link, and run the program. Record and try to explain what happens when you do so.

a. Change the declaration of *Deck* in file "CARDDECK.H" so that its private array of cards is declared as:
```
Cards card[52];
```

b. Look at the definition of function *Dealer::Shuffle* in file "DEALER.CPP". Change the header of the second `for` loop to read:
```
for (int j=0; j<=52; j++)
```

c. In the definition of function *Deck::Deck*, change the expression
```
cards[i].SetVal()
```
to read:
```
cards[i].val
```

d. In the definition of function *Dealer::StartHand*, change the second assignment statement to read:
```
d.numCards=0;
```

e. Remove the
```
friend class Dealer;
```
declaration from the declaration of class *Player*.

2. [Use the original versions of the PIP files for the following exercises.] We talked in the text about the support C++ offers for incremental testing. Let's write a simple driver program to test out specifically our declarations and definitions of cards and decks.

    a. Create a program file named "TESTPIP5.CPP" and enter `#include` directives for files "CARDDECK.H" and < iostream.h>.

    b. In the space provided below, write expressions that describe each of the following. Assume that we have declared a *Deck* named *d*:

        (1) the suit of the first card of the deck

        (2) the value of the second card of the deck

        (3) the value of the last card of the deck

    c. Now, add a `main` function to file "TESTPIP5.CPP" that creates a card deck, and prints the values of the above expressions on the screen. Compile and run your driver program, and explain its output.

    d. Extend your driver program so that it includes the statement
```
cout << cards[52].GetVal();
```
Try running your program, and explain what happens.

    e. Now, declare a function named *ShowDeck()* and make it a private member of class *Deck*. The definition of *ShowDeck()* should be in file "CARDDECK.CPP". Define *ShowDeck* so that it uses *Card*'s *Display* function to display each card in a deck. Compile your new versions of file "CARDDECK.H" and "CARDDECK.CPP".

    f. Finally, modify your driver program so that it calls function *ShowDeck* to display a newly created deck, instead of displaying the cards on its own.

g. Now that you're convinced that your *ShowDeck* function works properly, let's return to the original main function (as defined in "PIP5.CPP") and use it as the basis for extending our program further. We can, for example, use our *ShowDeck* function to demonstrate that when we create a *Dealer* object (and implicitly invoked *Dealer*'s constructor function) we are in fact creating a player and a card deck as well. Change function *Dealer::Dealer* so that it displays an entire deck before it is shuffled. Then, have it display the deck again after shuffling. (As an added bonus, this will tell us whether or not the function *Shuffle* is working.)

3. The following three proposed changes to our PIP are in fact quite independent from one another. You can try any or all of them. They are related in that each involves a seemingly substantive change to the program that can be made relatively directly. That is, the design of our program makes it easy to extend and modify the program by clearly distinguishing each logical entity and its processing activities.

a. Change your PIP so that it plays its game with two decks of cards. That is, play should continue until two decks (104 cards) have been dealt, one after the other. Before rushing off to a computer, think carefully about which classes and which functions this change affects.

b. Extend the program to implement a "5-card Charlie." That is, if any hand (the dealer's or the player's) contains 5 cards and still has a total value of less than or equal to 21, the hand is considered a winner (the equivalent of a hand with value 21).

c. Finally, let's take a step toward making our PIP at least a bit more general. Notice how both the player and the dealer in our game have a "hand." That is, the information about a hand (the array to store the cards, the current number of cards, the functions to determine the hand's value and to display the hand) are (nearly) duplicated in the declarations of both the *Player* and *Dealer* classes. Define a class *Hand* and then revise classes *Player* and *Dealer* to use it.

Postlab Exercises

1 . Our blackjack game is not totally realistic in the following sense. In an official game, aces can assume one of two values: eleven as in our version, or one. It is up to the holder of a hand (the player or the dealer) to choose which value should be used for the ace in determining the total value of the hand. Fix the program so that it allows for this flexibility.

2. Extend the program so that it resembles more closely a blackjack game as played at a table in a casino. That is, imagine that the dealer controls the play at a table, and that the table can seat up to 6 players. Each player, as in a casino, plays against the dealer using the same rules for dealing that we described earlier. When a game is completed (say, after four decks of cards have been dealt), the dealer should report the final pots of all players.

3 . Make the PIP's performance more visually appealing by extending it to display cards in graphical form. While graphical facilities vary from machine to machine (and from one C++ implementation to another), every environment supports some form (even text-based) of graphical display. Find out what is available on your system, and change the PIP so that it takes advantage of whatever display mode is available.

4 . Write a detailed, English description of how you could change this PIP to make it more useful to a wider range of card games. That is, describe how this PIP could be made to serve as a C++ "card game library."

Chapter 6
Pointers and References

Introduction

We covered a wide range of related topics in Chapter 6 of the text, and that leaves us with plenty to investigate in this lab. Pointers, references, and dynamic storage allocation are concepts that are difficult to express in many languages and so are often discussed at the end of an introductory programming course, if at all. These notions, though, are so important and so well supported by C++ that we can talk about them at this juncture, and then use them to our programming advantage throughout the rest of the course.

The common underlying theme in this diverse set of topics is that C++ gives us two fundamental ways to control how storage is allocated to our programs. We can predetermine the types and amount of storage our program needs, and leave it up to C++ to control that storage as our program passes through its various scopes. Or, we can say, as we do in this chapter's PIP, that we don't know ahead of time how much storage our program will require (since it is dependent in large part on how the program is used). In this latter case, we can choose to exercise more explicit control over how storage is allocated to our program. To do this, we need to develop our programming facility with pointers, references, and the `new` and `delete` operators. This lab is designed to help you do so.

Lab Objectives

In this lab, you will:
- Run the Chapter 6 PIP, an automated phone directory, noting its use of dynamic memory allocation to meet changing storage requirements.
- Analyze the PIP, paying careful attention to its use of references and destructor functions.
- Modify the PIP by performing functional decomposition on some of its existing functions.
- Extend the PIP to be even more efficient in terms of its memory allocation.

Exercises

1. We'll start, as usual, by compiling, linking, and running our PIP. As described in the text, the PIP consists of five files that declare, define, and use classes *Entry* and *Directory*. We will focus initially on how the program explicitly controls the size of a directory.

   a. Run PIP 6 now, being sure to make use of each of the available menu commands. Create a few entries, remove one, update another, and display the current directory.

   b. Quit the program for the moment, so that we can quickly edit one of our class definitions. Insert the following statement into the definition of function *Directory::DisplayDirectory* (in file "FONEBOOK.CPP") immediately before its if statement:

   ```
   cout << "Current maximum directory size: " << maxSize << '\n';
   ```

   c. Now, recompile the PIP, and run it. Create exactly five entries, and then display the directory. The program should indicate a maximum directory size of 5.

d. Add a new entry and watch what happens to the maximum directory size. What function was invoked to cause this change?

e. To get some further insight into our program's use of memory, let's see what its storage requirements really are. We could ask you to keep creating directory entries (or, to type in the Los Angeles phone book) until your computer refused to accept any more, but there's a quicker way.

   The constructor function for class *Directory* allocates a new directory of arbitrary size 5. Let's change the value of member data *maxSize*, and see how large a directory we can create. Change the value of *maxSize* in the definition of *Directory::Directory* to, say, 100, and rerun your program. You don't even need to create any entries. Just display the directory and you'll see if your machine allowed you to create one large enough to hold 100 entries.

f. Now, repeat the above process, each time setting maxSize to a bigger value (try 500, 1000, 10000, 100000,...). Record the point at which your program fails, and write down the error message that it produces (if it produces one at all!).

2. Let's shift our attention now to some of the other new and interesting features of the PIP. As we have done in previous labs, we will ask you to save original versions of each of the PIP's five files, and to make the changes we suggest below one at a time to the original versions of the PIP. On a separate sheet of paper, record for each suggested change whether or not the revised program ran, what error (if any) was produced, what type of error was produced (was the error detected by the compiler, the linker, or at runtime?), and an explanation of the resulting behavior. As before, the files to be edited are indicated in parentheses.

a. Remove the `include` directive for class *iostream.h* (in "ENTRY.H").

b. Remove the & following *Entry* in the header for overloaded operator >> (in "ENTRY.H" and "ENTRY.CPP").

c. Change all occurrences of -1 to zeroes (0), thereby changing function *FindName* to return a value of 0 when it cannot find a particular name in the directory ("FONEBOOK.CPP").

d. Declare and define the following destructor function for class *Entry* ("ENTRY.H" and "ENTRY.CPP"):

```
Entry::~Entry()
{
    delete name;
    delete phoneNumber;
    delete address;
}
```

3. Now, return to the original version of the PIP files so that we can extend the program in some useful ways. First, you'll modify the definition of class *Directory* so that it performs output a bit more directly. In particular, declare and define an overloaded insertion operator << for class *Directory*. That is, instead of having a function named *Directory::DisplayDirectory*, write a "friendly" output operator overload for << that displays a directory (d) by simply executing the statement cout << d. You can make use of the code already written for function *DisplayDirectory*.

4. In Chapter 6 of the text we talk about "functional decomposition." This is the process whereby complex functions are broken down ("decomposed") into smaller, simpler ones. Functional decomposition is useful in situations where a particular function is too long and detailed to be easily understood. In such cases, we can define one or more smaller functions to perform detailed processing, and rewrite the original function to invoke the newer, smaller ones. Another situation that dictates the use of functional decomposition is when more than one function all perform some common processing task. In this case, it is often useful to write a separate function that performs the processing that is common to the other functions, and to revise each of the other functions to call the new one.

Each of the following program extensions can be seen to result from one of these types of functional decomposition. Make each modification described. Then, run and test your new program.

a. Notice how functions *Remove*, *Lookup*, and *Update* from class *Directory* all begin by performing the identical process of prompting for and reading a name. Write a separate function, *ReadName*, that performs this processing, and modify each of three original functions to use it.

b. Write a separate function to accomplish the "shifting down" of an array, as described in function *Directory::Remove*. Modify *Directory::Remove* to call your *ShiftArrayDown* function.

c. Write a separate function called *CopyArray* that can be invoked from function *Directory::Grow* (and will be useful in the next exercise, as well) to transfer the contents of one array to another. The function should accept two arrays as its arguments.

5. Our final program extension makes use of some of the changes described above, and applies them to the task, once again, of making our program efficient with respect to its use of memory. The original PIP was written to recognize when it needed to "grow" its directory, and did so using the C++ new operator. Conversely, one can imagine having the program recognize when its directory is too large—say, in the case where less than half of its maximum number of entries are used. This can be implemented as follows.

a. Declare and define a function *Directory::Shrink()* to cut the maximum directory size in half. The *Shrink* function can make use of function *CopyArray*, as described in exercise 4, above.

b. Modify function *Directory::Remove* to act like *Directory::Insert*. That is, fix *Remove* to recognize when fewer than half of the current entries are being used and, in that case, to invoke your *Shrink* function.

c. Revise and compile your program to implement these changes. Before running your program, describe—in English— a simple procedure for testing it to see if your changes are working. Follow your test plan when running your revised program.

Postlab Exercises

1. Much of the processing described in program file "PIP6.CPP" is similar to that we described in class *User* in the Chapter 4 PIP. Revise PIP 6 to make use of a modified version of class *User*.

2. Write a function *Directory::ShiftArrayUp*, analogous to the *ShiftArrayDown* function described in exercise 4, above, that moves elements of an array "up" one position, leaving a blank entry at some specified location. Then, modify function *Directory::Insert* so that it maintains the phone directory in alphabetical order.

Chapter 7
Process I: Organizing and Controlling Classes

Introduction

Although we made a point of introducing no new features of C++ in this chapter, we still covered a lot of material related to the more general topic of computer programming. Mostly, we discussed our DDU approach to program development, and how it applies to this chapter's PIP, an elevator simulation. We described the DDU approach as one that supports the development of "workable," as opposed to merely "working," programs. A workable program, according to our description, is one that not only works, but also lends itself to the full range of software engineering activities that a program is typically subjected to. Our intention in this set of lab exercises is to demonstrate firsthand the workability of this chapter's PIP.

In particular, we will read through the source code to assess its readability and clarity. Then, we will point out some errors that can occur when running the program, and see if it can be easily debugged. After performing some experiments with our program's linkage, we will try to accomplish a few modifications and extensions to the program. Our hope is that the relative ease with which these activities can be performed will convince you that both the DDU approach and the C++ language are powerful and useful problem-solving tools.

Lab Objectives

In this lab, you will:
- Read carefully through, and then run, this chapter's PIP, an elevator simulation.
- Answer some questions about the program's organization and algorithms, based upon your understanding of the program.
- Run the program so as to produce some incorrect behavior, and debug the program to eliminate the source of the problem.
- Make some localized modifications to function definitions, and see that the changes do not affect the overall performance of the program.
- Extend the program by changing its design and its implementation.

Exercises

1. We start this lab by asking you to read a program, and we do so for two reasons. The first is that the version of the PIP that is distributed on your lab disk is slightly different than the one listed in the text. The disk version incorporates all of the proposed changes we suggested at the end of the text chapter. In particular, it includes changes to the header files for both classes *Elevator* and *Rider* to increase the program's protection of private members, and also makes use of functions *WaitForUser* and *Terminate* from the "UTILITY" file that we developed earlier.

    The second reason we want you to read the source code listing carefully is to demonstrate its readability. You should, after looking it over, understand the program well enough to work with it and manipulate it as we will ask you to do throughout the rest of this lab.

    a. Read through the complete program now, including the header and implementation files for classes *Elevator* and *Rider*, and the main program (from file "PIP7.CPP").

    b. Before proceeding to the next exercise, make sure you understand the program well enough to identify the specific line(s) in the source code that accomplishes each of the following processing steps.

(1) turns off an elevator's floor button when a rider gets off the elevator
(2) hails the elevator for a new rider
(3) changes the direction that the elevator is heading in
(4) decides that a rider is to get off the elevator

2. Having read and understood the program, we can now begin to work with it. Let's run the program and watch it handle a variety of riders and requests.

a. Run the program as distributed, entering whatever destination floor numbers you wish for each of the four riders. Make sure that all riders get served, and that they get served in the order you expect them to.

b. Change the `main` function so that more than four riders get created and served by the elevator. You will have to declare some additional riders (like those declared near the beginning of function `main`), and will have to modify the function's while loop to allow each of your additional riders to respond to the elevator's actions. When you are convinced that the elevator works properly for more than four riders at a time, leave the `main` function in its original form.

c. Run the original program again, this time providing bogus values as input when you are requested to supply destination floor numbers for each customer. That is, enter numbers that are either greater than or less than the number of floors in our simulated building. Record the inputs you supply and the program's output.

3. We asked you to run the program with out-of-range floor numbers to point out a weakness of our program. In some C++ environments, the program may produce a run-time error as a result of trying to reference a floor button that doesn't exist. In other environments, the program runs without detecting an error, but produces strange output (indicating, for example, that some customers were picked up but never served).

a. Run the program many times, providing out-of-range floor values for each run. Record carefully what inputs were provided, and what behavior resulted.

b. Using the information gathered above, devise a plan to keep this type of behavior from occurring. That is, decide which definitions need to be revised, and how they should be revised. Then, make the changes and verify that they work as you had hoped.

c. As a result of the above investigation, you may have noticed one other strange behavior of our original program. If it runs to completion, it reports that all riders have been served whether they have been or not. Revise function main so that the "having processed all requests" message only gets displayed if in fact the elevator served all riders.

4. In the text, we did our best to explain how C++ links programs that are composed from many distinct files. In particular, we showed a simple technique that uses the C++ preprocessor to avoid multiple definitions of external objects. The header files for the classes in this chapter's PIP, "ELEVATE.H" and "RIDER.H", both make use of this technique—and with good reason. Various functions in files "RIDER.CPP" and in "PIP7.CPP" refer to declarations from header file "ELEVATE.H". Also, file "ELEVATE.H" contains some simple definitions in addition to its class declaration. With some minor editing, we can show you what would happen if we have not taken any precautions to protect file "ELEVATE.H".

a. Clearly, file "PIP7.CPP" refers to declarations from file "ELEVATE.H". Currently it gains access to these declarations by including file "RIDER.H", which in turn includes our *Elevator* header file. What if, in writing function main, you didn't know that by including the *Rider* header file you would also get the *Elevator* header? You might be inclined, and rightfully so, to include the Elevator header file directly in your main program. Do so now. That is, edit file "PIP7.CPP" to include file "ELEVATE.H".

b. Now, edit file "ELEVATE.H" so that it does not make use of the preprocessor directives `#ifndef`, `#define`, and `#endif`. (Probably the easiest way to do this, since we will want these commands reinserted later, is to place comment symbols at the beginning of those lines.)

c. Run your program as edited and watch what happens when C++ tries to link your files together. Put your program back in its original state before continuing.

5. We'll now see how our design holds up when we are asked to undertake some reasonably straightforward modifications to our program. If our design is worth its salt, you should be able to accomplish either or both of the modifications below without major disruption to the declarations of any classes, and without affecting adversely the behavior of the program.

a. Notice that in function `main`, we print out the status values of each rider at the conclusion of the program. We do so to verify that all riders had been served. In the header file for class *Rider* we declared a rider's status to be an enumerated type, with values WAITING, ABOARD, and SERVED. Unfortunately, C++ has no provisions for displaying enumerated types directly. In fact, you probably noticed that the status values that get displayed at the end of our program are the integral values for the enumerated type (0, 1, and 2). Declare and define a new member function for class *Rider*, named *DisplayStatus*, that prints a rider's status in a more readable form. Then, modify function `main` to use *DisplayStatus*.

b. Notice, also in function `main`, how each instance of class *Rider* is declared. We use the C++ random number generator to produce a starting floor number, and then implicitly invoke *Rider*'s constructor function to initialize the rider accordingly. Modify *Rider*'s constructor so that it produces a random floor number for each rider internally, and doesn't have to rely on the main program to do so. This will necessitate that you change the constructor's parameter list, and also that you rearrange which of our program files includes which C++ library files.

6. Finally, we'll suggest a few slightly more dramatic program extensions. As above, you can try either or both. They are quite independent from one another conceptually and, hopefully, this will be reflected in our code. We leave it to you to determine which parts of the program require modification, to decide what those modifications should be, and to test your extended programs fully.

   a. One of the presumptions stated in our original program specification for this PIP was that our elevator had no maximum capacity. As you saw in an earlier exercise, you can create any number of riders, and our elevator never complains. Let's take a step towards making our program a bit more realistic. Change the program so that an elevator has a predetermined maximum capacity. The implication of this to a rider is that a rider cannot board the elevator if it is already filled to capacity.

   b. Functions *Elevator:ChooseMove* and *Rider::Respond* are somewhat simplistic, as well. You have probably already noticed that a rider will automatically get on the elevator when it stops at the rider's starting floor, even when the elevator is heading in the wrong direction for the rider. This is a result of the fact that our elevator does not distinguish between rider requests to go up and rider requests to travel down. It simply stops at every floor from which a request is made. Change the program so that:
   (1) When riders hail the elevator, they indicate which direction they want to travel, and
   (2) The elevator stops at a floor to pick up a rider only if there is one waiting there who is interested in travelling in the current direction. The elevator can, of course, stop to drop riders off and can also choose to change direction to accommodate a request.

Postlab Exercises

1. Use our elevator PIP as the basis for a program that simulates a "bank of elevators."

2. Programs like this PIP are called "simulations," in part because they can be used to simulate the behavior and performance of some real-world entity. This program could, for example, be expanded to help us to evaluate if one of our elevators could serve the expected traffic in a particular building. Extend this program to perform a more detailed simulation. It should determine values like: the number of riders served, the average number of riders on the elevator at any point in time, the average amount of time a rider spends on the elevator (as measured, perhaps, in moves from floor to floor), and the number of moves it takes to satisfy a random group of requests.

Chapter 8
Inheritance

Introduction

As we saw in the text, our PIP for this chapter is interesting from a variety of design and programming perspectives. Derived classes let us relate classes explicitly to one another in natural, expressive, and efficient forms. As you would expect, doing so introduces an organizational complexity to our programs that requires extra programming care.

In this lab we'll explore how inheritance affects working with a program. We'll see, for example, how changes in one class definition can cause errors in other parts of a program, and how extensions to a class can dictate changes to others. Ultimately, of course, we hope you'll develop the programming experience that will help you to work effectively with derived classes, so that you can exploit them and use them to your advantage.

Lab Objectives

In this lab, you will:
- Run and verify the output of this chapter's PIP, a payroll program.
- Perform a number of experiments that illustrate how the classes of the *Employee* hierarchy are related to one another.
- Modify the PIP so that it better exploits the inheritance features of C++.
- Extend the *Employee* hierarchy to describe two additional derived classes.

Exercises

1. We start, as usual, by compiling and running the PIP. As described in the text, you will need copies of three files ("EMPLOYEE.H", "EMPLOYEE.CPP", and "PIP8.CPP") to do so. You will also need to make sure that inline function *ClearScreen*, defined in "PIP8.CPP", is customized to your particular C++ environment.

   Do this now. You can either look through your C++ libraries for a function that accomplishes the clearing of the screen, or you can ask your instructor which function you should use and which library file it is declared in. Change file "PIP8.CPP" to reflect your findings, and run the program to make sure it works as it should.

2. Now that our program produces intelligible output, let's run it a few times to make sure that the output is correct. After creating three predefined employee checks (one each for a *Temporary*, *Hourly*, and *Salaried* employee), function `main` solicits data from the user describing three additional employees.

   Run the program a few times, providing different payroll data for these employees. Make sure that the checks produced correctly reflect both the type of employee being described and the data values entered. For example, the net pay for a temporary employee who worked 30 hours at a rate of $5.00 per hour should be $150.00. An hourly employee who worked the same hours at the same rate would receive only $50, and a salaried employee whose weekly pay is $500.00 would take home $400.00.

3. We can now experiment with our PIP to show how the hierarchy of *Employee* classes relate to one another. As we have done in previous labs, we'll propose a series of changes to make to the program (indicating which file is to be changed), and ask you to record what happens when you try to run the program. On a separate sheet of paper, describe whether the program ran or not, and if not, what type of error was reported. Then, write a sentence describing why the error occurred. Remember, as before, the suggested changes are independent from one another. That is, make all changes to the original working version of the program.

a. Change the declaration of class *Employee* so that member *netPay* is declared as `public` ("EMPLOYEE.H").

b. Change the declaration of class *Employee* so that member function *PrintCheck* is declared as `protected` ("EMPLOYEE.H").

c. Change the declaration of class *Employee* so that member function *PrintCheck* is declared as `private` ("EMPLOYEE.H").

d. Change the header of the declaration of class *Temporary* to read ("EMPLOYEE.H")

```
class Temporary: private Employee;
```

e. Change function `main` so that it includes the statement ("PIP8.CPP")

```
cout << h.name;
```

f. Change function `main` so that it includes the statement ("PIP8.CPP")

```
cout << t.hoursWorked;
```

g. Remove the initialization list from the parameterized constructor for class *Hourly* (*Hourly::Hourly*) ("EMPLOYEE.CPP").

h. Change functions *Employee::PrintCheck* and *Permanent::PrintCheck* so that they are not virtual functions. That is, remove the word `virtual` from their declarations and define them to have empty bodies (`{ }`) ("EMPLOYEE.H").

4. There are a number of natural extensions that can be made to our PIP. Some make the program more concise, some make it more efficient, and others extend its functionality. We described three extensions below, one of each type. Again, they are relatively independent from one another, so you can attempt to implement any or all of them.

   a. Looking at the function definitions in file "EMPLOYEE.CPP" we see three different sections of identical code to print the basic employee information in check form. This redundant code is a clear signal that we could probably do a better job of organizing our code. Try writing a function to print the basic information for all checks, call it *PrintCheckInfo*, and make it a member of class *Employee*. Then, modify the overwritten version of *PrintCheck* to call function *PrintCheckInfo*. (Notice, if you do this properly you can declare *Employee* member data items *name*, *address*, and *socSecNumber* as `private` to class *Employee*.)

b. Declare and define a virtual function named *CalculatePay* that performs the necessary calculation of value *netPay* for each *Employee* subclass.

c. Extend the *Employee* class hierarchy so that class *Temporary* serves as a base class for two derived classes, *Contract* and *Consultant*. *Contract* employees are *Temporary* employees who work for an hourly rate (like the *Temporary* employees in our original hierarchy). *Consultants* are *Temporary* employees who work for a fixed, flat rate. Rewrite function `main` to print checks for these new types of *Employee*.

Postlab Exercises

1. Describe a general class *VendingMachine* from which, for example, we could derive our class *SodaMachine* from the Chapter 3 PIP.

2. Write a class description to describe any small portion of the animal kingdom that you are familiar with (household pets, dogs, cats, horses, fish). Write a main program that creates animals of different kinds and displays their properties as they are created.

Chapter 9
Process II: Working with Classes

Introduction

Chapter 9 is about working with classes. In particular, it describes techniques for building programs from libraries and for debugging and extending programs, and applies them to the chapter's PIP. PIP 9 is a simple line-oriented word processor. In this lab we'll work more directly with a slightly different version of our PIP to help you to further develop your debugging and programming skills.

After exploring the debugging support provided by your C++ environment, we ask you to debug a version of the PIP that contains a variety of errors, some of which may require considerable effort to track down. Once the original PIP is running as intended, we ask you to extend it in a few obvious, but non-trivial ways. It is our expectation that in the process of doing so you will be confronted with problems of your own devising, providing you with yet another—and extremely realistic—opportunity to test further your debugging skills.

Lab Objectives

In this lab, you will:
- Explore the automated debugging support provided by your C++ environment.
- Debug versions of our PIP, a word processing program.
- Extend the PIP to provide additional editing and error-handling features.
- Extend the *OCString* class to provide additional operators on strings.

Exercises

1. We start, once again, by sending you off to do something on your own. Your do-it-yourself (or, at least, do-it-with-the-help-of-your-instructor) task is to familiarize yourself with the debugging support provided by your programming environment. You may even have to refer to a manual that is specific to your version of C++ to determine the range of operations that it provides. Many environments, for example, allow you to control the rate of execution of your program (moving, say, one statement at a time), to set breakpoints (instructions at which execution will temporarily halt, and from which it can be resumed), and to watch the values of specific variables and expressions as they change during execution.

   Ask your instructor for more information about the debugging facilities available to you, and then practice using them. They will certainly come in handy when working on the remaining lab exercises, and in all of your programming efforts. As we described in the text, being a good programmer depends in large part on being a good debugger, and good debuggers know how to make the most of modern, automated debugging tools.

2. Let's test out your debugging skills by asking you to track down one of the logical errors we intentionally introduced into the version of the PIP that was included on your lab disk. There is an error in the program that we want you to detect, find, and eliminate.

   Run the program as distributed and observe the output carefully. Then, re-read the section of Chapter 9 that describes what this program is supposed to do. It may also help to read carefully the two function definitions in file "PIP9.CPP". One final hint: After inserting a few lines into a new document, try displaying the document on the screen.

3. Having succeeded in fixing the PIP, you can now extend the program in a number of simple ways. We group the changes according to which library or file they affect most directly. It is up to you (and to your instructor!) to choose which exercises you will undertake. There's plenty to choose from.

Exercises a-c relate most directly to function main *and files "PIP9.CPP"
and/or "USER2.CPP".*

a. Write a separate function, named *CleanUp*, which can be called from
function main to save the current document after editing has been
completed.

b. Write a separate function, named *StartUp*, which can be called from
function main to open an existing document file before the program begins
its editing loop.

c. Change the program so that the opening and saving of documents are not
done automatically when the program starts and ends. Instead, make
"open" and "save" menu commands that can be invoked at any time by the
user.

*Exercises d-g relate most directly to the declarations and definitions of class
Document in files "DOCUMENT.H" and "DOCUMENT.CPP".*

d. Write a separate (private) function for soliciting a file name from the user
of a program that can be called from functions *Document::Retrieve* and
Document::Save.

e. Change function *Document::Insert* so that it allows many lines to be
inserted after a single insert command. The function should continue to
read and insert lines until an empty line (which should not be recorded in the
document) is entered by the user.

f. Overload the insertion and extraction operators for class *Document*. That
is, redefine the operators so that an entire document can be read from or sent
to any stream in a single statement.

g. As currently implemented, the first string in the text array for a document,
text[0], is intentionally left blank so that the user's counting scheme for line
numbers can jibe with the program's. We can use this space in a document
to store a "file signature"—that is, a sequence of characters that identifies

the document as one that can be processed by our program. Change the program so that it stores a special string (you pick one) in position zero of every document text array (the same string in each document!). Then, change the *Save* function to store this string as part of a document on disk, and change the *Retrieve* function so that it only reads files that begin with the chosen file signature.

Exercises h-k relate most directly to the declarations and definitions of class OCString, in files "OCSTRING.H" and "OCSTRING.CPP".

h. Add the statement
```
        cout << "Calling the OCString destructor";
```
to the destructor function for class *OCString*. Run the program, and count how many times this function is called.

i. Many C++ environments contain functions named *getLine* and *putLine* that read and write, respectively, C++ strings up to and including end-of-line markers. See if your environment provides such functions. If it does, rewrite (and simplify considerably) any *OCString* functions that could benefit from them.

j. Overload the assignment operator (for a second time) so that standard C++ strings can be assigned directly to *OCStrings*. Rewrite any portions of the program that could make use of this type of assignment.

k. Build into class *OCString*'s overloads of the extraction and insertion operators checks that detect when an attempted I/O operation on *OCStrings* fails. When an attempt at I/O fails, the user should be notified, and processing should continue.

Postlab Exercises

1. Extend the PIP so that two documents can be opened at once, with one of them being distinguished as the "current" document—that is, the one to which current editing operations apply. This likely will entail an additional menu command that allows the user to specify which of the documents is the current one.

2. Using the results for Postlab Exercise 1, extend the program one step further to allow for any number of open documents at a time.

3. Using our PIP as a model, try to write a character-oriented (as opposed to line-oriented) word processor. As with most modern word processors, yours should allow for a full range of operations on individual characters (perhaps as well as on lines as a whole).

Chapter 10
Algorithms

Introduction

The PIP for this chapter as presented in the text is not really a program at all, but rather a collection of related, but independent classes and functions. On your lab disk we have provided the C++ declarations and definitions for class *IntArray*, and for some of the sorting algorithms described in the text. We also provide a bare-bones `main` function that will allow you to begin running and experimenting with these algorithms. Your task in this lab will be to develop further the `main` function and to write another of your own to perform more extensive algorithm analysis on the sorting functions.

In particular, we ask you to write a driver program to test out implementation of class *IntArray*, to make sure it is as safe as we claim in the text. Then, you will be guided through a series of simple extensions to the sorting functions that will provide you with some concrete data in terms of which you can compare the algorithms for relative efficiency.

Lab Objectives

In this lab, you will:
*   Write a driver program to test our implementation of class *IntArray*.
*   Run this chapter's PIP to convince yourself that our C++ implementations of *InsertionSort*, *SelectionSort*, and *Quicksort* sort correctly.

- Modify the PIP to count the numbers of data comparisons and data movements performed by each of the sorting functions.
- Extend function `main` to gather and report more extensive data for comparing the sorting algorithms.

Exercises

1. Before we start looking at the functions that sort integer arrays, let's look more closely at our implementation of the arrays themselves. Class *IntArray*, as described in the text, offers what we regard as a somewhat safer implementation of arrays (integer arrays, in this case) than is provided directly by C++. Your job for the moment is to write a simple driver program that exercises class *IntArray*, and convinces you that it works properly and is as safe as advertised.

Specifically, write a `main` function that accomplishes the following:

a. creates a variety of *IntArray*s, using all four constructors,

b. verifies that each array created has the proper length and the expected data values,

c. assigns *IntArray*s to one another, and verifies that the assignment operator works, and

d. uses the subscript (selector) operator to access individual *IntArray* elements.

To check the safety of class *IntArray*, your driver program should also:

e. create an *IntArray* of size -1,

f. try accessing an element with the selector operator that is beyond the range of an *IntArray*,

g. apply the assignment operator to two *IntArrays* of different size.

2. Now that we have confidence in our implementation of class *IntArray*, we can turn our attention to the sorting functions that manipulate such arrays. We start by simply running the program described in file "PIP10.CPP". This file contains definitions for functions that implement the Insertion sort, Selection sort, and Quicksort algorithms presented in the text, as well as a simple `main` function.

Function `main` creates and initializes three identical *IntArrays*, applies a different sorting function to each, and displays the (hopefully) sorted versions of the arrays. Run this program a few times now, varying the value assigned variable size each time. Examine the output to make sure that each array is getting sorted properly.

3. Having answered the question "Are the arrays getting sorted properly?" we now turn to the pivotal question for this chapter: Are the arrays getting sorted efficiently? As we pointed out in the text, questions of algorithm efficiency are relative ones, even when comparing algorithms on a single machine. So, the best we can do to measure the relative efficiencies of our three sorting functions is to compare their performances to one another according to some criteria that reflect the effort expended to accomplish an identical sort.

If you look at each sorting function and strip away the `for` loops (which primarily iterate over other statements), most of what is left are data comparisons (either in `if` or `while` statements) and calls to UTILITY function *Swap*. So, the two criteria we will use (for the moment) are the number of data comparisons performed and the number of data movements made by each function. Edit file "PIP10.CPP" as follows so that we can begin to evaluate the efficiency of our sorting functions:

a. Declare six variables of type `long`, to represent the number of data comparisons and data swaps for each of the three sorting functions. For example,

```
long      insertionComps, insertionSwaps,
          selectionComps, selectionSwaps,
          quickcomps,     quickSwaps;
```

Place these declarations at the beginning of file "PIP10.CPP" (*not* in function main—you'll see why shortly).

b. Initialize all 6 of these variables to zero at the beginning of function main.

c. Modify functions *InsertionSort*, *SelectionSort*, and *Partition* (because of the modifications we'll make to *Partition*, function *Quicksort* need not be modified) to increment the appropriate counter variables whenever comparisons or swaps of *IntArray* data are performed, as below.

```
void InsertionSort(IntArray& a, int p, int r)
{
   for (int i=p+1; i <= r; i++)
   {
      int j=1;
      while ((j > p) && (a[j] < a[j-1]))
      {
         insertionComps++               // ADD THIS STATEMENT
         insertionSwaps++;              // ADD THIS STATEMENT
         Swap(a[j], a[j-i]);
         j--;
      }
   }
}
void SelectionSort(IntArray& a, int p, int r)
{
   for (int i=p; i < r; i++)
   {
      int min = a[i], where=i;
      for (int j=i+1; j <= r; j++)
      {
         selectionComps++;              // ADD THIS STATEMENT
         if (a[j] < min)
         {
            min = a[j];
            where = j;
```

```
            }
            Swap(a[j], a[where]);
            selectionSwaps++;                // ADD THIS STATEMENT
        }
    }
}

int Partition(IntArray& a, int p, int r)
{
    int top = r+1, bottom = p-1;
    int pivot = a[p];
    while (top > bottom)
    {
        do
        {
            bottom++;
            quickComps++;                    // ADD THIS STATEMENT
        } while (a[bottom] < pivot);
        do
        {
            top--;
            quickComps++;                    // ADD THIS STATEMENT
        } while (a[top] > pivot);
        Swap(a[top], a[bottom]);
        quickSwaps++;                        // ADD THIS STATEMENT
    }
    Swap(a[top], a[bottom]);
    quickSwaps++;                            // ADD THIS STATEMENT
    return top;
}
```

d. Modify function main so that instead of displaying the sorted versions of
   each array (which are identical, anyway), it displays the values of the six
   counter variables after all sorts have been performed.

4. To get a more realistic picture of the relative performances of our three
   algorithms, our main program should exercise them more rigorously, and on a
   wider range of data. The main program provided below does so, and requires
   no changes be made to our sorting functions. Edit file "PIP10.CPP" now so

that function main appears as follows.

```
void main()
{
    Randomize();
    for (int size=500; size<=2000; size += 500)
    {
        // vary the sizes of the arrays to be sorted
        IntArray a(size), b(size), c(size);

        // initialize all comparison and swap counters
        insertionSwaps = 0;
        insertionComps = 0;
        selectionSwaps = 0;
        selectionComps = 0;
        quickSwaps = 0;
        quickComps = 0;

        for (int runs = 0; runs < 5; runs++)
        // for each array size, build and sort 5 examples
        BuildArray(a, size);
        c = b = a;

        InsertionSort(c, 0, size-1);
        SelectionSort(b, 0, size-1);
        QuickSort(a, 0, size-1);

        cout << "\n\nArray size: " << size << "\n\n";
        cout << "\nAverages for Insertion sort: "
                << insertionSwaps / runs
                << insertionComps / runs;
        cout << "\nAverages for Selection sort: "
                << selectionSwaps / runs
                << selectionComps / runs;
        cout << "\nAverages for Quick sort: "
                << quickSwaps / runs
                << quickComps / runs;
    }
}
```

5. Run the revised PIP, and record the numbers reported for comparisons and swaps for each sorting function. Produce, by hand, a graph that shows the average number of swaps measured against the array data size for all three algorithms. Do the same for the average number of comparisons. Describe your findings in terms of the big-O descriptions of these algorithms in the text.

Postlab Exercises

1. Below is an informal description of the *Shellsort*, named after its inventor, D. L. Shell:

```
interval = size / 2;
do
{
    for (i=0; i , interval; i++)
    {
        // use InsertionSort to sort array elements i,
        // i+interval, i+ (2*interval), i+(3*interval) . . .
        interval /= 2;
    }
} while (interval != 0)
```

Implement this algorithm as a C++ function, and add the function definition to file "PIP10.CPP". Extend function `main` to call, test, and analyze the *Shellsort* function in the same way we have analyzed the other three sorting functions.

2. Another perhaps even more direct way to measure the speed of an algorithm is to actually time it. Most C++ environments provide a collection of functions that allow one to check the time on the system clock from within a program. By checking the time at two locations (say, one before a function is called and one after the function returns) we can get an approximate measure of the processing time that expired between those locations. Check out the timing functions available to you (start by looking in library header file <time.h>), and revise "PIP10.CPP" to perform a timing analysis of the sorting algorithms.

3. Now that we have sorting functions ready to use, we can perform an analysis of the basic searching algorithms we described in the text. Use the functions and techniques illustrated in "PIP10.CPP" to analyze the relative efficiencies of the linear and the binary search algorithms.

Chapter 11
Classes in the Abstract

Introduction

This text chapter introduces the topic of Abstract Data Types (ADTs), with an emphasis on the "Abstract," and in so doing broadens out programming perspectives considerably. Classes can now be seen as even more general entities by virtue of the fact that they can be parameterized for type. We no longer need to constrain ourselves to thinking in terms, say, of lists of integers, lists of floats, and lists of strings. We can, at this new level of abstraction, just think about lists. Furthermore, we can couple the notion of parameterized classes with our well-established habit of distinguishing declaration files from definition files to achieve a heretofore unattainable level of programming flexibility. By declaring and defining parameterized classes according to our standard format, it becomes realistic—and easy—to consider alternative implementations for classes, and to compare different implementations as to their suitability to a particular problem. This is precisely what we'll do in this final set of lab exercises.

Specifically, we will complete and extend the two implementations of lists described in the text. Then, we'll write a simple driver program that, by editing one of its characters, can be used to exercise both list implementations. The powerful notions of object-oriented programming, abstract data types, and C++ all combine to afford us this tremendous programming flexibility.

This final PIP, like most of the others we have seen, comes to you in pieces. On your lab disk we have provided you with a header and definitions file for an array-based List ADT ("AList") and a header and definition file for a linked-list version of a List ADT ("LList"). As in the previous chapter, these files are related, but do not fit together to form a cohesive program. Rather, we will experiment with and use them in a variety of combinations to gain an appreciation for the degree to which C++ supports the development of ADTs.

Lab Objectives

In this lab, you will:
- Complete and extend the two implementations of the List ADT described in the text.
- Write a driver program to exercise both implementations of the List ADT.
- Extend both implementations of the List ADT to provide additional functionality.
- Compare the relative performance of the two implementations of lists.

Exercises

1. We start by looking at the array-based implementation of our List ADT. Let's write a driver program to exercise it. Like any good driver program, yours should invoke each member function (including all available constructors), should access representative data members, and should insure that the class is behaving as expected. Write, test, and run a complete driver program for class TList (as declared in file "ALIST.H") now.

2. In our description of the linked-list version of the List ADT in the text, we intentionally left function *Remove* undefined. We did, though, explain its operation in detail in Section 11.3. Re-read that description now. Then, write a definition for function *TList::Remove*, and add it to file "LLIST.CPP".

3. The driver program you wrote for Exercise 1, above, no doubt included file "ALIST.H". By changing that directive to #include "LLIST.H", we can use the same driver program to exercise our linked version of the List ADT. Do so now, and check carefully that the driver program performs exactly as it did in

Exercise 1.[2]

4. Extend both implementations of class *TList* to include an *Append* function that inserts a new element after the last element of a list. Extend your driver program to test function *Append*, and run it on both List implementations.

5. We mention in the text that the ways in which a program is used, or the types of data involved, can dictate that one implementation of an ADT is more efficient than another. Compare the running times of the *Append* function on lists of a variety of sizes for the two implementations of class TList. Which implementation would you prefer if your program frequently invoked *Append* to operate on very large lists?

Postlab Exercises

1. In the PIP from Chapter 9, the word processor program, we described a document as a list of *OCStrings*. Rewrite PIP 9 using the List ADT.

---

[2] Some C++ implementations require that the definition file be included when a class is parameterized, like AList is. In this case, your include statement must read: `#include "ALIST.CPP"`.